Dr. William Harvey

AND THE DISCOVERY OF CIRCULATION

Science Story Library

Dr. William Harvey

AND THE DISCOVERY OF CIRCULATION

by William C. Harrison

illustrated by Laszlo Kubinyi

THE MACMILLAN COMPANY • NEW YORK

COLLIER-MACMILLAN LIMITED • LONDON

The Macmillan Company, New York
Collier-Macmillan Canada, Ltd., Toronto, Ontario
Library of Congress catalog card number: AC 67-10267
Printed in the United States of America
First Printing

Dr. William Harvey

AND THE DISCOVERY OF CIRCULATION

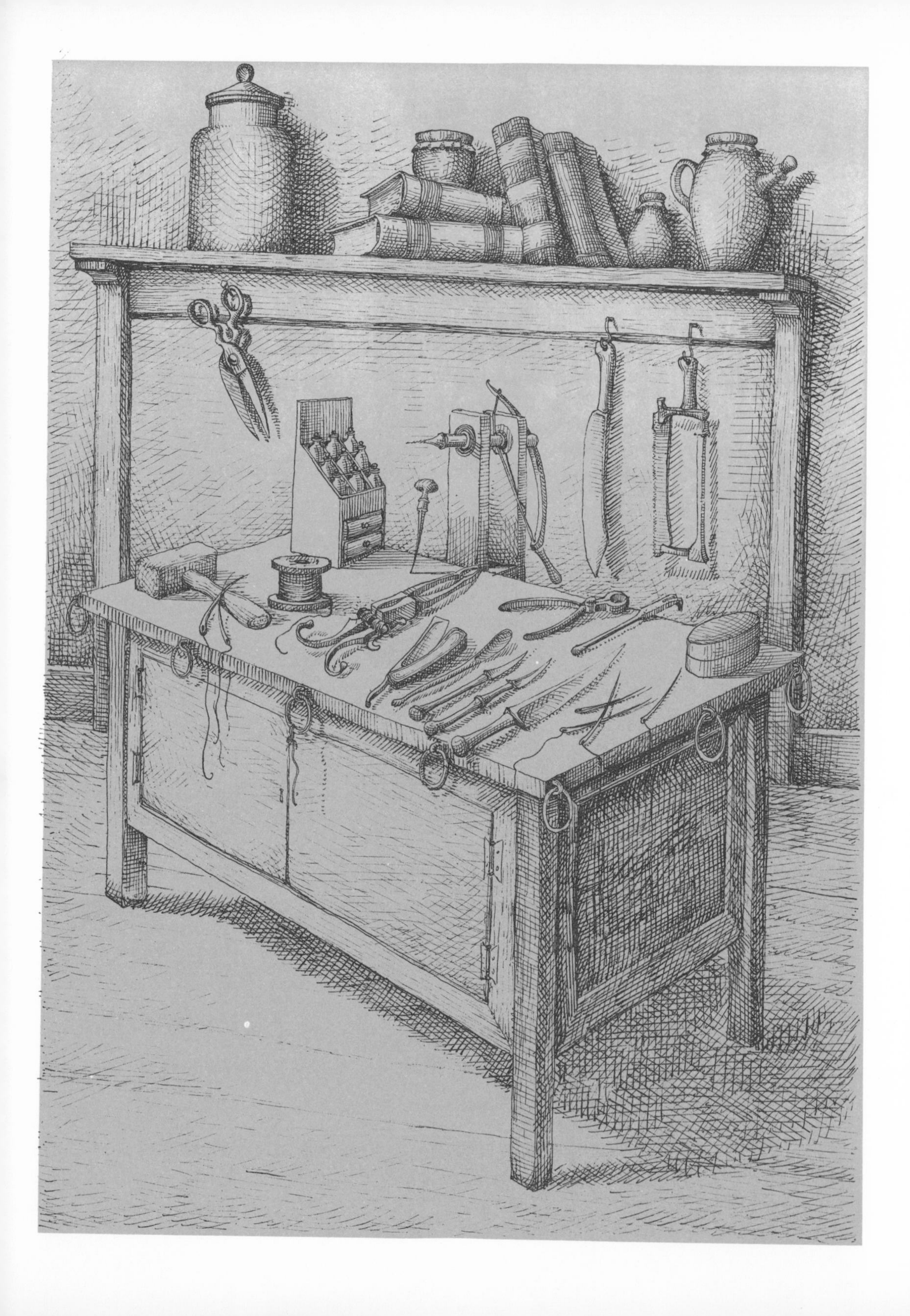

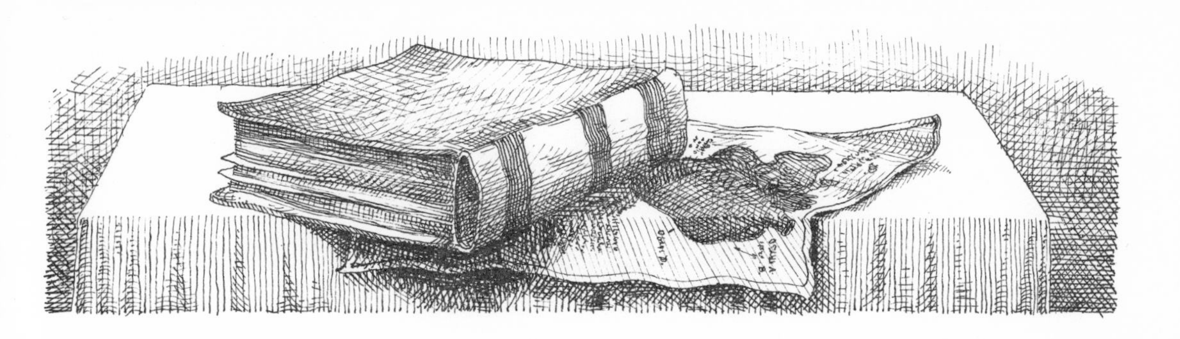

PRESS YOUR HAND against your chest. Can you feel your heart beat? Perhaps you can count the pulse in your wrist as doctors and nurses do. The throbbing you can feel with your fingers is also caused by the movements of your heart.

Man has probably been aware of his heartbeat since prehistoric times when people lived in caves. But it is only in the last 350 years that we have come to understand how the heart's movements direct the circulation of the blood. We owe this knowledge to a doctor-scientist named William Harvey, who unlocked the secrets of the heart.

Your heart is almost tireless, endlessly pumping every minute of your life. The work the muscular little organ does each day is enough to lift your body a mile into the air. The rate of beating changes to meet varying requirements. For example, when you have been running or playing hard you can feel your heart pounding faster. That is because your muscles have been working and need more food and oxygen. The blood carries this nourishment to the cells of your muscles and conducts waste material to the kidneys.

An adult has an estimated 60,000 miles of blood vessels carrying this vital fluid to all the cells in the body —each and every one dependent on the heart. The circulating blood does much more than carry food, oxygen, and waste products. Certain glands in the body manufacture chemicals called hormones, which regulate such life processes as reproduction and growth. The glands release the hormones into the bloodstream, which then carries them wherever they are needed. The blood also carries the materials that fight germs and help the body to repair injured tissues. And it cools us by removing excess heat from deep within our bodies to the skin, where it passes harmlessly into the air.

Our understanding of these and many other functions of the heart and blood stems from the discoveries Dr. Harvey made. And from this understanding have grown countless life-saving techniques of modern medicine. The transfusion of blood from one person to another is an example.

William Harvey was born on April 1, 1578, the first of nine children of Thomas and Joan Harvey. Mr. Harvey was a well-to-do official of Folkestone, a town

on the southeast coast of England. In Folkestone you are always aware of the sea and, when the weather is clear, you can see France, twenty-five miles away, across the English Channel.

As a child, William liked to play by the shore on warm summer days. He began to ask questions as soon as he learned to talk. He asked more questions than all of his brothers and sisters together.

"Where do the ships come from?"

"What makes waves, and why are they sometimes big and sometimes small?"

"How do sea gulls fly?"

The boy was curious about everything he saw. He would run after the retreating surf with the breezes ruffling his jet-black hair. Snatching up green and white pebbles and pink shells as he ran, he would then ask questions about *them.*

Sometimes his father could not answer all his questions. Mr. Harvey would laugh and say, "When you are

ten years old, I will send you to a fine school so you can learn everything you want to know."

William became ten in an exciting year. His country and Spain were at war. A fleet of Spanish warships with big guns was sailing straight for England and Folkestone. Elected mayor by the townspeople, Mr. Harvey prepared the port for invasion.

But when the Spanish Armada, as the invading fleet was called, lay off Calais, a French port across the Strait of Dover, English ships attacked. The people of Folkestone could see smoke billowing above a furious battle. The Spanish ships carried larger cannons than the English ships, but their heavy shots dropped into the

water before reaching the English vessels. After a while the Armada's guns fell silent—the Spaniards had used up all their ammunition. The English then closed in with their smaller guns and sank many enemy ships. The rest of the Armada fled into the North Sea just as a storm arose. Battered by gale winds, less than half of the invading fleet were able to return to Spain.

A few weeks later when William's father took him to live with an uncle in Canterbury and to go to school there, the boy had thrilling stories to tell about the great sea battle.

Canterbury Grammar School was the oldest and one of the best in England, and William studied hard. He did so well that he was admitted to Gonville and Caius College, Cambridge, on a scholarship only two months after his fifteenth birthday. The scholarship paid his living expenses and allowed him to attend classes free.

The other boys and the teachers liked William. He was a good student, especially enjoying philosophy, the study of the principles underlying nature and human behavior. He also studied Greek and Latin. It was during these years at Cambridge that many of his questions began to be about medicine.

"What causes people to get sick?"

"How can a fever be cooled?"

"Why do some cuts heal quickly while others swell up, turn red, and take a long time to heal?"

William was smaller than most of the other boys his age, but energetic and quick-tempered. Bigger boys soon learned not to push their fiery classmate around. They found him good company. He always had something interesting to say and his curiosity was as wide as the world itself.

The student's day began with chapel at five o'clock in the morning—before daylight. Classes and study continued until nine-thirty at night—long after dark in the winter. Meals were skimpy and the rooms were cold. To get their feet warm before going to bed, the boys were made to run for half an hour between nine-thirty and ten. William often missed classes for long periods of time—probably made sick by the harsh conditions.

When he was graduated in 1597, at the age of nineteen, he was determined to become a doctor.

At that time the world center of medical education was the University of Padua in Italy, on the Continent and many hundreds of miles away. William asked his father for permission to go.

Mr. Harvey agreed that William should go to Italy even though it would be expensive. His other sons, he was sure, were not as interested in an education and would rather work for merchants in the city. Indeed, they eventually became wealthy merchants themselves.

Padua was noted for love of learning, religious tolerance, international spirit, and freedom of thought. Experimental research was encouraged. Students and teachers came from many nations and freely traded ideas.

In those days students became followers of a particular teacher. William enrolled at Padua as a student of Fabricius, the leading anatomist of the time. An anatomist dissects, or takes apart, the different parts of bodies to study their position, their relationship to each other, and their structure and function. Doctors need this knowledge to enable them to treat the sick.

The young student from England observed dissections so carefully and eagerly that he soon became a favorite of the famous Fabricius, at times helping him with experiments.

The old teacher would call William from the gallery, where students stood to watch an anatomy demonstration, perhaps the dissection of a robber who had been caught and put to death.

"Come down here, William," Fabricius would say. "Please dissect a vein in this man's arm and show the little flood-gates [valves] inside that permit the blood to flow freely toward the heart but not so freely away from it."

When William received his doctor of medicine diploma with high honors at Padua on April 25, 1602, Fabricius himself signed the document. The young Englishman, he said, had been an outstanding student and showed promise of becoming a fine doctor.

ΓΙΑΤΡΩΣ
ΦΑΒΡΙΚΙΟΣ

Back in England, William was eager to start his career in London, the capital city. But his degree from Padua only allowed him to practice in other parts of England, and so he returned to his old school at Cambridge to obtain another medical degree. This made him eligible to join the College of Physicians in London—now called the Royal College of Physicians—and to practice medicine there.

Dr. Harvey began to treat the sick, and he soon had a busy practice. Many rich and prominent people came to him for care. But he was never too busy with his daily work to question and to study. He continued to make careful dissections and examinations just as he had before.

In 1604, Dr. Harvey married Elizabeth Browne, daughter of Dr. Lancelot Browne, physician to King James I. We know little about Mrs. Harvey except that she was a tall woman—probably taller than her husband—with a dark complexion and a rather severe look. We also know that she owned a pet parrot.

The bird was handsome and a famous talker. It was allowed to wander freely through the house. When Mrs. Harvey had been out, the parrot would fly to her when she returned, climb up her dress to her shoulder, then walk down her arm and settle on her hand. And it would sing and talk whenever it was asked.

The parrot eventually died in Mrs. Harvey's lap. Its death caused great sorrow to the young couple, for they had no children and they loved the talkative bird. Years later, in a notebook he kept, Dr. Harvey described their pet. "Playful and impudent," he wrote, "it would often seat itself in my wife's lap to have its head scratched and its back stroked, whilst a gentle movement of its wings and a soft murmur witnessed to the pleasure of its soul."

Because female parrots are usually quiet, the Harveys had thought their sociable pet to be a male. But when the parrot died, the doctor dissected its body and found an egg inside, showing it to have been a female. Dr. Harvey's careful notes about the bird were typical of the anatomical observations he made so diligently all his life.

A few years after his marriage, Dr. Harvey became an officer of the College of Physicians and its lecturer in anatomy and surgery, a position he was to hold for the rest of his life. He also became physician to St. Bartholomew's Hospital, a famous institution in London that still exists today.

As time went on, the British physician worked harder and harder and won more and more honors. And he asked more questions. But now he asked them

of himself, because no one else knew the answers.

In class lectures, Dr. Harvey showed his students and fellow physicians the little flood-gates in the veins that let the blood flow in *only one* direction. Even Dr. Harvey's old teacher, Fabricius of Padua, had failed to recognize the full function and significance of the valves he had found in the veins.

When the blood is in the veins, Harvey would point out, it is always moving toward the heart. The blood in the arteries, on the other hand, flows away from the heart. Then he would explain how the heart pumps the blood in circular paths—out through arteries to all parts of the body and back through veins to the heart again.

Nobody else had ever learned how the heart controls the circulation of the blood. Dr. Harvey had discovered this secret because he kept asking himself questions and continued making dissections until he found the answer he was seeking.

"Look," he would say to the doctors and students in the lecture room while showing them the exposed hearts of live animals. "See how the heart contracts like a closing fist to squeeze the blood into the arteries, and then relaxes to fill again from the veins."

The most famous physicians who had ever lived taught things about the heart and blood that were different from what Dr. Harvey had found in years of careful dissections, experiments, and observations.

There was the ancient Greek Hippocrates, respected as the father of medicine. Followers of Hippocrates believed that blood vessels carried air and other substances in addition to blood. The real function of the heart was unknown. Aristotle, another scientist-philosopher of ancient Greece, had taught that the blood was made in the liver from food. Aristotle also taught that the heart instead of the brain was the seat of intelligence. None of these things was true, but even centuries later they were widely believed.

There was the great Galen, physician to the Roman Emperor Marcus Aurelius. Galen's writings during the second century A.D. ruled medicine for 1,400 years. He taught that blood passed directly from one chamber of the heart, the right ventricle, to the opposite chamber, the left ventricle, by seeping through tiny holes or

pores in the wall separating them. This single false notion—accepted everywhere as true—blocked medical progress for centuries. Galen also said—mistakenly—that the blood ebbed back and forth in the body like ocean tides.

And there was Andreas Vesalius of Padua, the founder of modern anatomy. When only twenty-eight

years old, he produced a beautifully illustrated anatomy textbook based on what he had found in making his own dissections, not on what Galen, Hippocrates, Aristotle, and other learned men had taught. Overturning the anatomical authority of more than a thousand years, Vesalius boldly announced that Galen's "pores" between the heart chambers did not exist.

It was not a popular announcement. People refused to believe that Galen could be wrong. Discouraged and abused, Vesalius burned his other writings, left Padua, and produced little else of importance for the rest of his life.

Dr. Harvey knew how angry people would be if he, too, wrote a book saying that the old and trusted authorities were wrong. He realized that expressing new ideas, even though they were true, could be dangerous. Harvey knew of many men who had been punished for their beliefs.

Even the world-famed genius Galileo, who had taught science at Padua when young Harvey was a student there, was later denounced and persecuted for proclaiming great new truths about the earth, sun, and stars. Galileo, by then a sick old man, was imprisoned and forced to deny what he knew to be true.

Nevertheless, with the urging and encouragement of

his friends, Dr. Harvey bravely resolved to write a book setting down what he had learned about the heart and the blood. But the doctor was also a thorough scientist. Before writing the book, he wanted to check and re-check his experiments to make certain that they were correct in every detail. And there was one more thing he needed to find out about the blood-flow circle: just how did the blood pass from the distant ends of the arteries into the distant ends of the veins to return to the heart? How was that gap in the circle bridged?

Dr. Harvey kept on demonstrating to his students and colleagues his discovery of the heart's function and the circular passage of blood throughout the body.

"Observe carefully," he would say. "Consult your own senses. Don't just accept what I say. Rely on what you find yourself; don't depend on someone else. Wise men must learn from the fabric of Nature herself, not from the decrees of other men."

He repeatedly urged his students not to guess, but to seek the truth in dissections. Dr. Harvey himself never tired of studying the anatomies of dogs, pigs, snakes, frogs, fishes, snails, oysters, lobsters, insects, unhatched chicks, and, of course, people.

Finally in 1628, twelve years after his first lecture on the circulation of the blood, Dr. Harvey published his book. It is usually known by its shortened Latin title, *De Motu Cordis.* These words mean "on the movement of the heart."

The book was short, only seventy-two pages. But it has often been called the most important medical work ever written. The book marks a high point in the history of human thought, laying the cornerstone of modern medicine. It also set forth, step-by-step, the scientific

method for learning facts about the body and how it functions.

Dr. Harvey was fifty when the book was published. Well known and highly regarded in medical circles, he was elected that year to be treasurer of the College of Physicians.

The expected storm of abuse then broke about his head. Other doctors called him crack-brained. They said he was wrong and Galen was right. Dr. Harvey said nothing. He let the book—and truth—speak for him. But many of his private patients left him because they had heard other doctors say that he held dangerous, new-fangled ideas.

Fortunately, however, Dr. Harvey found a strong friend in England's new king, Charles I, who became interested in the physician's discoveries.

"Demonstrate the circulation of the blood to my Royal Court," King Charles commanded.

Dr. Harvey cut open the fist-sized heart of an animal to show the king and his nobles the four hollow spaces within. He traced the route of the blood when it was carrying waste material, telling how it entered from the veins into one chamber called the right atrium and flowed through a valve or one-way gate into a second chamber called the right ventricle.

He explained how the heart beats, squeezing the blood out of the right ventricle through arteries to the lungs. (We now know the lungs cleanse the blood of waste carbon dioxide and furnish it with fresh oxygen from the air we breathe.)

"The bright red blood," Dr. Harvey explained, "then returns to the left side of the heart or left atrium. Then it goes through another one-way valve into the fourth chamber or left ventricle. From there, by the squeezing movement I mentioned, the blood is pumped out through arteries to nourish all parts of the body. Eventually, it comes back to the heart again, continually flowing in a kind of circle."

"It is clear that you are right," said King Charles. "But how does the blood that has flowed out through the arteries get into the veins to return to the heart?"

Dr. Harvey admitted that he did not know how this happened, although he was convinced that it was true. "The blood steals into the veins and flows back everywhere through those very veins," he said. "I will keep on trying to find the hidden part of its pathway that must be there."

In the meantime King Charles appointed Harvey Physician to the King and the Royal Household, which more than made up for the patients who had left him.

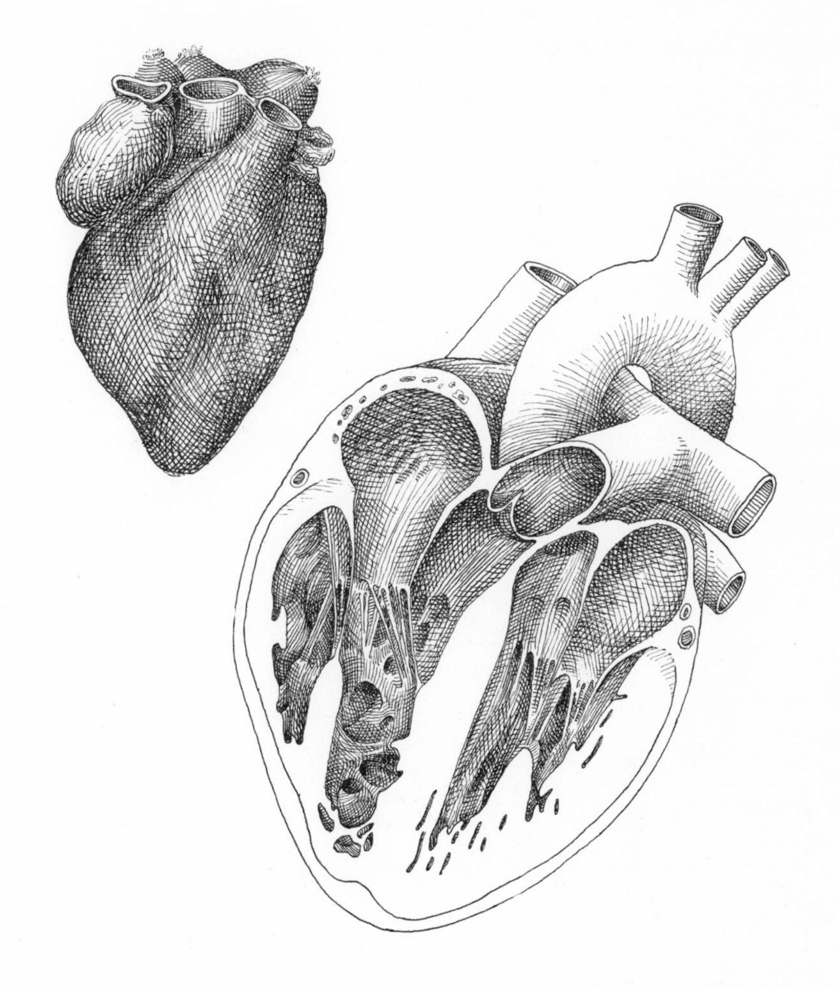

In fact, King Charles liked Dr. Harvey so much that he gave him a large oil portrait of his oldest son, Charles, the Prince of Wales, and sent the doctor on important missions to other nations. He also asked Dr. Harvey to handle some unusual medical examinations for

him. Once Harvey saved the lives of four women who were threatened with death. A ten-year-old boy had lied about the women and made people believe they were witches. In those days anyone convicted as a witch was burned to death.

The boy had played truant—been absent from school without permission—and had made up a wild tale to avoid punishment. He said one of the women had grabbed him and carried him swiftly through the air over fields, bogs, and rivers to a large barn. She led him inside by the hand, he said, where seven old women were pulling at seven animal halters hanging from the roof. Out of the halters fell chunks of meat and butter, loaves of bread, pans of milk, and two kinds of puddings. More witches came, and everybody ate supper on the barn floor, the boy insisted—"and that was the reason I didn't go to school."

Of course, the story was completely false, but the boy stuck to it, even repeating it in church. When he came out, he pointed to some women he claimed he had seen in the barn. Many were arrested and some were charged with being witches.

Because people believed that witches could be identified by special signs on their bodies. King Charles ordered Dr. Harvey to examine the women. The physician was too wise to believe that they were witches but he did as the king commanded.

"They are just like other women," he reported. "They have nothing unnatural on their bodies." And so the women were pardoned by the king.

On another occasion, at the king's bidding, Dr. Harvey performed an autopsy—or examination after death

—on a man named Thomas "Old" Parr, who had lived to be almost one hundred and fifty-three.

The king wanted to know why the old man had finally died.

Dr. Harvey checked the body thoroughly, outside and inside. He found the man's organs remarkably healthy.

The physician then explained to King Charles that Thomas Parr had been a poor countryman who breathed pure air and ate only such plain food as cheese, bread, and milk. But a nobleman had recently brought him to London, where the air was smoky and bad. The city people gave him all kinds of rich food and drink he was not used to.

"The change proved too much for him," Dr. Harvey reported. "If his usual habits had not been interfered with, he might have lived some time longer."

Wherever King Charles went, Dr. Harvey went too. Even when the king got into a bitter quarrel with Parliament, the group of men who helped him to rule England, and left London, Dr. Harvey accompanied him.

Soon civil war broke out all over the kingdom. King Charles and his army were fighting Parliament and its army.

At the Battle of Edgehill, the first major clash of the war, Dr. Harvey tended the wounded. A writer of the time named Aubrey said the physician also took care of the king's two sons, the Prince of Wales, aged twelve, and the Duke of York, aged ten. Dr. Harvey took the

two boys under a hedge near the battlefield, pulled a book from his pocket, and began reading. But, said Aubrey, the shot of a big gun grazed the ground near them, and they had to scurry to a safer place.

Meanwhile, Parliament dismissed Dr. Harvey from

his position at St. Bartholomew's Hospital, where he had served for about thirty-five years. And in London, a mob of Parliament soldiers broke into Dr. Harvey's quarters, stole his furniture, and destroyed notes covering years of experiments and observations.

The doctor, in describing the action years later, said that he was attending the king "not only by the leave but at the order of Parliament" when the mob broke into his house and looted it. Nothing was so crucifying to him as the loss of his papers, he said.

The fighting went on. King Charles had set up his court at Oxford, and Dr. Harvey settled down to scientific work and teaching at Merton College there. The king appointed him head of the school.

Dr. Harvey's stay at Merton College was short, but it resulted in a warm and enduring friendship with one of his students, Charles Scarborough.

Scarborough was thirty-eight years younger than his teacher. In much the same way that Harvey had helped Fabricius with experiments in anatomy, Scarborough now helped Harvey. And just as Harvey had become famous, so did Scarborough. He went on to become a leading anatomist and doctor and was knighted in 1669.

The two men remained close and lifelong friends. The older man willed to the younger his velvet doctor's gown and "all his little silver instruments of surgery."

In 1646, the king fled Oxford, but was captured. He escaped, only to be seized again and beheaded.

With the surrender of Oxford and the capture of the

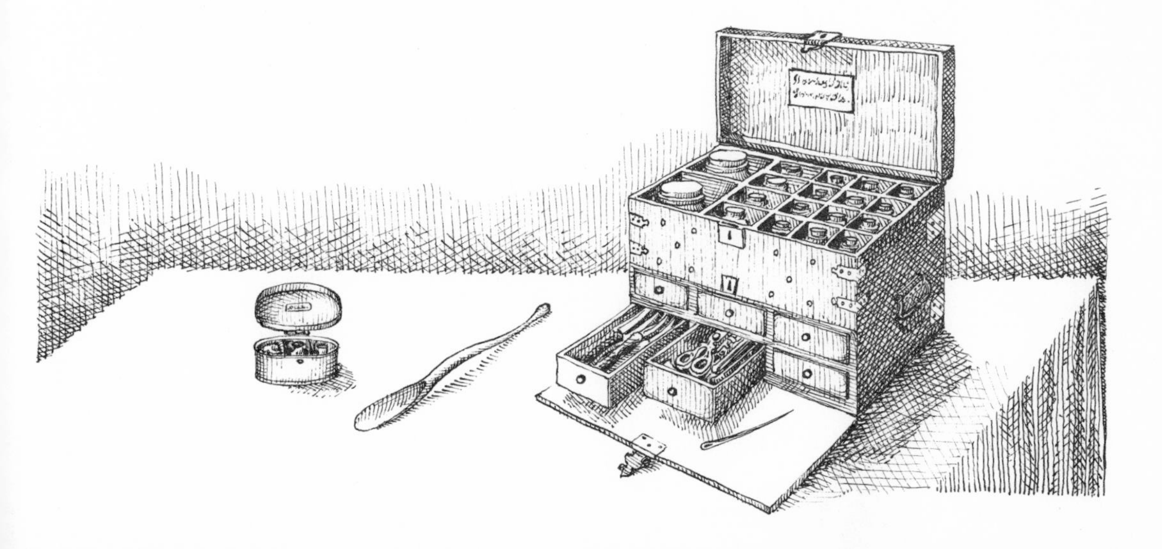

king, Dr. Harvey, now sixty-eight years old, was allowed to return to London. His wife had died, and since they had had no children, he lived at the homes of his brothers. He suffered from gout, a disease that caused him intense pain in the legs and feet. Sometimes he would get up in the night and sit on the flat roof of the house, putting his feet in a pail of cold water "till he was almost dead with cold" to make the pain go away.

The doctor was no longer able to practice medicine, but he continued his scientific studies, nonetheless. He had workmen dig caves in which he liked to sit in the summertime and think. The caves were cool and quiet.

At Christmas in 1650, when Dr. Harvey was seventy-two, an old friend and fellow physician, Dr. George Ent, came to visit.

"I found him intent on examining the nature of things . . . with a cheerful countenance and a quick mind," Dr. Ent related. "And eager to talk of dissections."

"I have always thought it right to look at the animals themselves," Dr. Harvey said, "and I have imagined that we could obtain from them not only some of the lesser secrets of Nature, but even some inkling of the Supreme Creator himself. And, though many things were discovered by learned men of yore, I should

imagine that many more are still buried in the dark night of unexplored Nature.

"I have indeed often wondered or even laughed at those who believe that everything has been so perfected and completed by Aristotle, Galen, or some other great person that not a single jot can be added to his account."

Impressed as always by Dr. Harvey's wisdom, Dr. Ent told his old friend that other men awaited his further experiments.

Dr. Harvey smiled and said, "Do you really wish once again to send me out into the treacherous sea away from the peace of this haven in which I pass my life? You know well how much trouble my earlier studies evoked."

But despite his fears, Dr. Harvey had not been idle. He showed Dr. Ent a manuscript he had been working on ever since his days at Padua.

Dr. Ent begged for permission to assemble the work and publish it and offered to correct the proofs and see them through the print shop.

Dr. Harvey pointed out that one whole section was missing because the notes had been destroyed by looters during the civil war. But he finally agreed that Dr. Ent might have the manuscript.

The result was another important book, this one about the generation of animals, the processes by which they produce their young. The notes he had made about his wife's pet parrot fifty years before were included in the book.

Dr. Ent took great trouble to prevent mistakes in the work—not always an easy task.

"Our author," he said, "is wont to write such a fist that no one without practice can easily read it."

Dr. Harvey did, in fact, scribble such a mixture of English and Latin that it was sometimes almost impossible to unravel what he had meant to say. His spell-

ing was occasionally strange, too—the word "piggg" appears in one place in his notes, as though he had the animal by its curly tail and could not let go.

Long before Dr. Harvey's book on generation was published, the world had recognized that he was a great man. His findings about how the heart circulates the blood were being taught in the best universities. A statue of him was erected at the College of Physicians, and in 1654 its members unanimously chose him to be their president. The doctor thanked them for the honor but declined the post, saying he was too old and ill.

Dr. Harvey loved the College and provided it with a handsome building for a library and museum. Later, in July, 1656, he gave a magnificent banquet for the members of the College and presented it with another valuable gift—the deeds to an estate he owned.

The next year, on the morning of June 3, Harvey was stricken with paralysis. He sent for his brothers and nephews and gave each of them something to remember him by. Later that day he died, in his eightieth year.

A great-niece of Dr. Harvey said many years later that in his old age her famous uncle developed some rather odd habits. She reported, for instance, that he came to prefer sugar to salt on his food and so kept his saltcellar filled with sugar. And when he had made up his mind to have dinner at a certain time, he would sit down and eat even if expected company had not yet arrived. The great-niece also related that "He used to walk out in a morning, combing his hair in the fields." Perhaps the doctor was still preoccupied with the problem he had never been able to solve—the missing link between the arteries that carried the blood away from the heart and the veins through which it returned.

It was not until 1661, four years after Dr. Harvey's death, that an Italian named Marcello Malpighi found the answer the doctor had sought so long. Looking through a microscope at the lung tissues of a frog, Malpighi discovered the tiny blood vessels we call capillaries that connect the arteries and the veins.

Dr. Harvey was unable to discover the capillaries because the crude lenses available during his lifetime were not powerful enough to reveal them. These vessels are so tiny that if ten of them were put into a bundle it would be no thicker than a hair.

With better equipment, the persistent English scientist would surely have discovered the capillary link between the arteries and the veins. As it was, he found where the gap in his theories existed and bridged it with imagination and logic.

INDEX